Collins

Reading Comprehension Progress Tests

Year 4 / P5

Author:
Josh Lury

Series editor:
Stephanie Austwick

William Collins's dream of knowledge for all began with the publication of his first book in 1819.

A self-educated mill worker, he not only enriched millions of lives, but also founded a flourishing publishing house. Today, staying true to this spirit, Collins books are packed with inspiration, innovation and practical expertise. They place you at the centre of a world of possibility and give you exactly what you need to explore it.

Collins. Freedom to teach.

Published by Collins
An imprint of HarperCollinsPublishers
The News Building
1 London Bridge Street
London
SE1 9GF

Browse the complete Collins catalogue at
www.collins.co.uk

© HarperCollinsPublishers Limited 2019

10 9 8 7 6 5 4 3 2 1

ISBN 978-0-00-833345-4

British Library Cataloguing-in-Publication Data

A catalogue record for this publication is available from the British Library.

Author: Josh Lury

Series editor: Stephanie Austwick

Publisher: Katie Sergeant

Product Manager: Catherine Martin

Development editor: Judith Walters

Copyeditor and typesetter: Hugh Hillyard-Parker

Proofreader: Catherine Dakin

Cover designers: The Big Mountain

Production controller: Katharine Willard

Printed and bound by CPI Group (UK) Ltd, Croydon, CR0 4YY

The publishers gratefully acknowledge the permission granted to reproduce the copyright material in this book. Every effort has been made to trace copyright holders and to obtain their permission for the use of copyright material. The publishers will gladly receive any information enabling them to rectify any error or omission at the first opportunity.

TEXT

An extract on pp.7-8 from *The Dragon's Bride and Other Dragon Stories* reprinted by permission of HarperCollins Publishers Ltd © Fiona Macdonald 2017; An extract on pp.9-10 from *Super Stars* by Jenny Vaughan reprinted by permission of HarperCollins Publishers Ltd © HarperCollins Publishers Ltd 2016; An extract on pp.16-17 from *Welcome to My City* by Charlotte Raby reprinted by permission of HarperCollins Publishers Ltd © HarperCollins Publishers Ltd 2017; An extract on p.18 from *The Butterfly Lion* reprinted by permission of HarperCollins Publishers Ltd © Michael Morpurgo 1996; An extract on pp.33-34 from *Your Brain* by Sally Morgan reprinted by permission of HarperCollins Publishers Ltd © HarperCollins Publishers Ltd 2013; An extract on p.35 from *Little Wolf's Book of Badness* reprinted by permission of HarperCollins Publishers Ltd © Ian Whybrow 1995; An extract on pp.41-42 from *Mr Stink* reprinted by permission of HarperCollins Publishers Ltd © David Walliams 2009; An extract on pp.52-53 from *A Dog Called Homeless* reprinted by permission of HarperCollins Publishers Ltd © Sarah Lean 2012.

IMAGES

p.7 Illustration by Fiona Macdonald reprinted by permission of HarperCollins Publishers Ltd © HarperCollins Publishers Ltd 2017; p.9 Illustration by Martin Bustamante reprinted by permission of HarperCollins Publishers Ltd © HarperCollins Publishers Ltd 2016; p.16t Illustration by William Alvarez (Sylvie Poggio Artists) reprinted by permission of HarperCollins Publishers Ltd © HarperCollins Publishers Ltd 2017; p.16bl Illustration by William Alvarez (Sylvie Poggio Artists) reprinted by permission of HarperCollins Publishers Ltd © HarperCollins Publishers Ltd 2017; p.16br Illustration by William Alvarez (Sylvie Poggio Artists) reprinted by permission of HarperCollins Publishers Ltd © HarperCollins Publishers Ltd 2017; p.17t Illustration by William Alvarez (Sylvie Poggio Artists) reprinted by permission of HarperCollins Publishers Ltd © HarperCollins Publishers Ltd 2017; p.17b Illustration by William Alvarez (Sylvie Poggio Artists) reprinted by permission of HarperCollins Publishers Ltd © HarperCollins Publishers Ltd 2017; p.18 Reprinted by permission of HarperCollins Publishers Ltd © Christian Birmingham 1996; p.24 SSSCCC/Shutterstock; p.26t Sararoom Design/Shutterstock; p.26b JaySi/Shutterstock; p.27t Cherkas/Shutterstock; p.27b ChiccoDodiFC/Shutterstock; p.33t Ella197/Shutterstock; p.33b Illustration by Laszlo Veres reprinted by permission of HarperCollins Publishers Ltd © HarperCollins Publishers Ltd 2013; p.34 Golden Pixels LLC/Shutterstock; p.35 © HarperCollins Publishers Ltd 2019; p.41 Reprinted by permission of HarperCollins Publishers Ltd © Quentin Blake 2009; p.43 kyslynskahal/Shutterstock; p.50 Baiajaku/Shutterstock; p.52 Reprinted by permission of HarperCollins Publishers Ltd © Gary Blythe 2012.

Contents

How to use this book

Introduction

Collins *Reading Comprehension Progress Tests* have been designed to give you a consistent whole-school approach to teaching and assessing reading comprehension. Each photocopiable book covers the required reading comprehension objectives from the 2014 Primary English National Curriculum. For teachers in Scotland, the books can offer guidance and structure that is not provided in the Curriculum for Excellence Experiences and Outcomes or Benchmarks.

As standalone tests, independent of any teaching and learning scheme, the Collins *Reading Comprehension Progress Tests* provide a structured way to assess progress in reading comprehension skills, to help you identify areas for development, and to provide evidence towards expectations for each year group.

Assessment of higher order reading skills

At the end of Key Stage 1 and Key Stage 2, children are assessed on their ability to demonstrate reading comprehension. This is done through national tests (SATs) accompanied by teacher assessment. Collins *Reading Comprehension Progress Tests* have been designed to provide children with opportunities to explore a range of texts, whilst building familiarity with the format, language and style of the SATs. Using the tests with your classes each half-term will offer you a snapshot of your pupils' progress throughout the year.

The tests draw on a wide range of text types, from original stories and poems to engaging non-fiction material. The questions follow the style and format of SATs papers at a level appropriate to the year group, and the tests provide increasing challenge within each year group and across the school. Through regular use of the progress tests, children should develop and practise the necessary skills required to complete the national tests confidently and proficiently.

How to use this book

In this book, you will find six photocopiable half-termly tests, written to replicate the format of the SATs. Each child will need a copy of the test. You will also find a Curriculum Map on page 6 indicating the aspects of the Content Domain covered in each test across the year group. These have been cross-referenced with the appropriate age-related statements from the National Curriculum.

The Year 4 tests demonstrate standard SATs-style questions and mirror the recognised KS2 format of whole texts followed by an answer booklet. Each test includes two contrasting texts. There is no set amount of time for completion of these tests but a guide is to allow approximately one minute per mark. However, the length of text increases in Tests 5 and 6 so it is important to develop children's reading stamina and fluency and teach them how to retrieve information quickly, efficiently and accurately.

To help you mark the tests, you will find mark schemes that include the number of marks to be awarded, model answers and a reference to the elements of the Content Domain covered by each question.

Test demand

The tests have been written to ensure smooth progression in children's reading comprehension within the book and across the rest of the books in the series. Each test builds on those before it so that children are guided towards the expectations of the SATs at the end of KS1 and KS2.

Year group	Test	Number of texts per test	Length of text per test	Number of marks per test
4	Autumn 1	2	300 words each or 600 words in total	20
4	Autumn 2	2	300 words each or 600 words in total	20
4	Spring 1	2	300 words each or 600 words in total	20
4	Spring 2	2	300 words each or 600 words in total	20
4	Summer 1	2	400 words each or 800 words in total	20
4	Summer 2	2	400 words each or 800 words in total	20

Performance thresholds

The table below provides guidance for assessing how children perform in the tests. Most children should achieve scores at or above the expected standard with some children working at greater depth and exceeding expectations for their year group. Whilst these threshold bands do not represent standardised scores, as in the end of key stage SATs, they will give an indication of how children are performing against the expected standard for their year group.

Year group	Test	Working towards	Expected	Greater Depth
4	Autumn 1	10 marks or below	11–15 marks	16–20 marks
4	Autumn 2	10 marks or below	11–15 marks	16–20 marks
4	Spring 1	10 marks or below	11–15 marks	16–20 marks
4	Spring 2	10 marks or below	11–15 marks	16–20 marks
4	Summer 1	10 marks or below	11–15 marks	16–20 marks
4	Summer 2	10 marks or below	11–15 marks	16–20 marks

Tracking progress

A record sheet is provided to help you illustrate to children the areas in which their reading comprehension is strong and where they need to develop. A spreadsheet tracker is also provided via **collins.co.uk/assessment/downloads** which enables you to identify whole-class patterns of attainment. This can be used to inform your next teaching and learning steps.

Editable download

All the files are available in Word and PDF format. Go to **collins.co.uk/assessment/downloads** to find instructions on how to download. The files are password protected and the password clue is included on the website. You will need to use the clue to locate the password in your book.

You can use these editable files to help you meet the specific needs of your class, whether that be by increasing or decreasing the challenge, by reducing the amount of questions, by providing more space for answers or increasing the size of text as required for specific children.

Year 4 Curriculum map: Yearly overview

National Curriculum objective (Year 4)	Content domain	Test 1		Test 2			Test 3	Test 4		Test 5		Test 6	
		Fiction	Non-fiction	Non-fiction	Fiction	Poetry	Non-fiction	Non-fiction	Fiction	Fiction	Poetry	Non-fiction	Fiction
Comment on words and phrases that capture the reader's interest and imagination.	2g Identify/explain how meaning is enhanced through choice of words and phrases.	•			•	•			•	•	•		•
Recognise some features of different forms of poetry.	n/a					•					•		
Explain the meaning of words in context.	2a Give/explain the meaning of words in context.	•	•	•	•	•	•	•	•	•	•	•	•
Draw inferences such as inferring characters' feelings, thoughts and motives from their actions, and justifying inferences with evidence.	2d Make inferences from the text / explain and justify inferences with evidence from the text.	•	•	•	•	•	•	•	•	•	•	•	•
Predict what might happen from details stated and implied.	2e Predict what might happen from details stated and implied.	•			•				•	•			•
Identify main ideas drawn from more than one paragraph (or verse) and summarise these.	2c Summarise main ideas from more than one paragraph.	•	•	•	•	•	•	•	•	•	•	•	•
Identify how language, structure and presentation contribute to meaning.	2g Identify/explain how meaning is enhanced through choice of words and phrases.	•	•	•	•	•	•	•	•	•	•	•	•
Retrieve and record information/identify key details from fiction and non-fiction texts.	2b Retrieve and record information / identify key details from fiction and non-fiction.		•	•			•	•				•	

The Dragon and His Granny

From *The Dragon's Bride and Other Dragon Stories* by Fiona Macdonald

Far away and long ago, there were three best friends. Their names were Jake, Will and Conrad. Jake was sensible. Will was a worrier. Conrad was daring. Times were tough in their home town and so they decided to run away together.

"We'll need to find jobs," said Jake.

"And food ... and shelter," said Will.

"Boring!" said Conrad. "I want to find fame and fortune and have adventures."

At first, all went well. But, by wintertime, the friends were in trouble. They were cold and wet – and homeless and hungry and frightened.

"Do you think we'll die?" groaned Will, as they sheltered under some bushes.

"Well, not right now," said Jake. "But ... WHAT'S THAT? HIDE! GET DOWN!"

Red, roaring flames lit up the world. There was hissing and sizzling and a terrible smell of burning.

Conrad was the first to look around. He could hardly believe his eyes. It was a real live dragon!

"Good afternoon!" the dragon said. "Why are you hiding?"

"Why do you think?" said Conrad. "We're scared!"

"We've never met a dragon before," explained Jake, rather more politely.

"It's your roaring I don't like," whispered Will.

"Why aren't you at home?" the dragon said, kindly. "Or at work, or at school?"

The friends told him.

"But I can help you!" the dragon replied. "Here's a magic wand. It makes gold. Try it!"

Amazed and excited, Conrad waved the wand, and sure enough, a pile of gold coins appeared at his feet.

"But beware!" said the dragon. "That wand comes with a terrible price."

"Take it back, then!" cried Will.

"Too late!" snarled the dragon. "Enjoy the gold! But in seven years' time, you must pay the price for my help. I'll make you my slaves – for ever!" Then he flapped his wicked wings and flew off into the sky.

Telescopes

From *Super Stars*
by Jenny Vaughan

Telescopes

Long ago, the only way people could see stars and planets was with the naked eye. But when telescopes were invented, around 500 years ago, everything changed. When anyone looked through a telescope, they could see far-away objects very clearly.

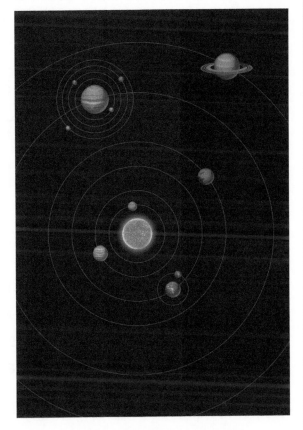

Galileo Galilei was an astronomer who lived in Italy between 1564–1642. He was one of the first scientists to point a telescope at the sky to study stars and planets.

Using a telescope, it was possible for Galileo and others to see stars and planets better than before, and to make new discoveries.

This is how Galileo saw the universe. The Sun is in the centre and the planets orbit around it.

For thousands of years, people had thought the Earth was in the centre of the universe, and the Sun, Moon, planets and stars surrounded it. Looking through a telescope, Galileo realised that the Earth is just one planet in orbit around a single star – the Sun. Beyond that, there's more space, and more stars than we can count.

The biggest telescope on Earth

Astronomers today still use telescopes, but many of them are much bigger and more powerful than the one Galileo used. The telescopes are built in places like the top of mountains, where the air is very clear and clean. From there, experts can get the best view of the stars with no pollution to get in the way.

The biggest ever telescope on Earth is being built in the Atacama Desert, Chile. It's called the European Extremely Large Telescope, or E-ELT. The E-ELT will give astronomers a better view of the stars and planets from Earth than ever before.

Telescopes in space

There are also telescopes in space, orbiting Earth. The Hubble Space Telescope has been working in space for over 20 years. It can see further than the telescopes on Earth, and it sends back clear pictures of the stars to scientists on the ground.

Name:	Class:	Date:

Questions 1–9 are about 'The Dragon and his Granny'
(pages 7–8).

1 Read the first paragraph. **Find** and **copy** a phrase that explains why the boys ran away from their homes.

_____

1 mark

2 Which word **best** completes the sentence about Conrad's personality?

✓ Tick **one**.

Conrad was a/an _____ sort of character.

calm ☐   adventurous ☐   older ☐

1 mark

3 *"We've never met a dragon before," explained Jake, rather more politely.*

Which word has a similar meaning to the word *rather* in this sentence from the story?

✓ Tick **one**.

angrily ☐

hardly ☐

kindly ☐

somewhat ☐

1 mark

4 *"Do you think we'll die?"* groaned Will

Explain the reasons for Will saying this.

_____

_____

_____

_____

2 marks

5 *"Why aren't you at home?"* the dragon said, kindly.

Put ticks (✓) in the table to show which of these are **true** and which are **false**.

	True	False
The dragon was hiding.		
The dragon was trying to trick the boys.		
The boys began to trust the dragon.		

1 mark

6 Find the part where the dragon *snarled*.

What does this show about how the dragon had changed?

_____

_____

_____

2 marks

7 *"That wand comes with a terrible price."*

What does *terrible price* refer to?

✓ Tick **one**.

lots of gold coins ☐

expensive clothes ☐

a cost to their freedom ☐

mistaken price ☐

1 mark

8 The boys' emotions change through the story.

Number the sentences below from **1** to **4** to show the order in which they happen.

They are afraid they won't survive the winter. ☐

They feel deceived. ☐

They trust the dragon. ☐

They are determined to find a new life. ☐

1 mark

9 What do you predict will happen in the next part of the story?

Read the story title carefully, and include that in your idea.

_____

_____

_____

_____

2 marks

Questions 10–15 are about '**Telescopes**' (pages 9–10).

10 When were telescopes first invented?

_____

1 mark

11 *Galilieo Galilei was an astronomer*

Find and **copy** a phrase from the text to explain what *astronomers* do.

_____

1 mark

12 Why are telescopes often built at the top of mountains?

✓ Tick **one**.

So not too many people visit. ☐

Most astronomers live on mountains. ☐

To avoid pollution. ☐

So no noise can distract the astronomers. ☐

1 mark

13 Give **two** reasons that the Hubble telescope is special.

1. _____

_____

2. _____

_____

2 marks

14 Find the part that describes the E-ELT.

What can you tell about the telescope from its full name?

_____

_____

_____

1 mark

15 Explain why Galileo's discovery may have shocked many people.

_____

_____

_____

_____

2 marks

Paris

From *Welcome to My City*
by Charlotte Raby

Paris

Paris is in a very low-lying area called the Paris Basin, which is shaped like a massive bowl. Paris is mostly flat – but there's one famous hill, Montmartre, that is 130 metres high.

Bonjour! I'm Manon, and I'm from Paris, the capital of France.

In prehistoric times, the Paris area was underwater. The shells and bones of sea creatures made the limestone and gypsum rocks beneath Paris.

From Roman times onwards, people have mined the limestone and gypsum for building materials and to make Plaster of Paris.

Who lives in Paris?

Population: over 2.2 million

Foreign tourists per year: over 15 million

Landscape

The river Seine wiggles through Paris, crossed by 37 bridges. The city has built up along the river.

There are two natural islands in the Seine – the Île de la Cité and the Île Saint Louis. The Île de la Cité is where Paris began! Long ago, before the Romans came, a Gallic tribe called the Parisi lived on this island. When the Romans arrived in 52 BCE, they built their city of Lutetia spreading out from the Île de la Cité.

Today, the Notre Dame Cathedral is on the island. It was built from the limestone mined beneath the city.

What's it like to live here?

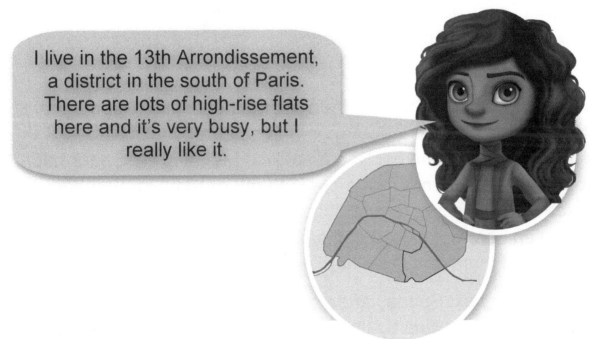

I live in the 13th Arrondissement, a district in the south of Paris. There are lots of high-rise flats here and it's very busy, but I really like it.

Many Chinese and Vietnamese people have immigrated to the 13th Arrondissement, and there are lots of Chinese and Vietnamese shops and restaurants.

You can find fruits like durian and rambutan, which aren't on sale anywhere else in Paris.

From *The Butterfly Lion*

by Michael Morpurgo

I was ten, and away at boarding school in deepest Wiltshire. I was far from home and I didn't want to be. It was a diet of Latin and stew and rugby and detentions and cross-country runs and chilblains and marks and squeaky beds and semolina pudding. And then there was Basher Beaumont who terrorised and tormented me, so that I lived every waking moment of my life in dread of him. I had often thought of running away, but only once ever plucked up the courage to do it.

I was homesick after a letter from my mother. Basher Beaumont had cornered me in the bootroom and smeared black shoe-polish in my hair. I had done badly in a spelling test, and Mr Carter had stood me in the corner with a book on my head all through the lesson – his favourite torture. I was more miserable than I had ever been before. I picked at the plaster in the wall, and determined there and then that I would run away.

I took off the next Sunday afternoon. With any luck I wouldn't be missed till supper, and by that time I'd be home, home and free. I climbed the fence at the bottom of the school park, behind the trees where I couldn't be seen. Then I ran for it. I ran as if bloodhounds were after me, not stopping till I was through Innocents Breach and out onto the road beyond. I had my escape all planned. I would walk to the station – it was only five miles or so – and catch the train to London. Then I'd take the underground home. I'd just walk in and tell them that I was never, ever going back.

Name: Class: Date:

Questions 1–8 are about 'Paris' (pages 16–17).

1   Why is Montmartre unusual in Paris?

_____

1 mark

2   **Find** and **copy** the phrase that shows what the rocks under the city are made from.

_____

1 mark

3   Who first mined the rocks under the city?

✓ Tick **one**.

sea creatures ☐

Romans ☐

prehistoric people ☐

Manon ☐

1 mark

4   Read the *Paris fact* about who lives in Paris.
Draw **two** lines to match the boxes below correctly.

visit Paris each year	over 2.2 million
live in Paris permanently	over 15 million

1 mark

5 Read the description of the main river in Paris.

✓ Tick **one** to complete the sentence to match the description in the text.

The Seine _____ through the city.

floods ☐   goes straight ☐   winds ☐

_____
1 mark

6 Number the sentences below from **1** to **3** to show the order in which different groups inhabited the area of Paris.

Romans   ☐

Parisi   ☐

Vietnamese immigrants   ☐

_____
1 mark

7 Read about the landscape of Paris.

Put ticks (✓) in the table to show which of these are **true** and which are **false**.

	True	False
The Romans named the town the Île de la Cité.		
Modern Paris has 37 bridges.		
Lutetia was built around the islands.		
Notre Dame is built beneath the city.		

_____
2 marks

8 Why do you think some people might travel to Manon's area of the city? Give **two** reasons based on the text.

1. _____

_____

2. _____

_____

2 marks

Questions 9–15 are about *The Butterfly Lion* (page 18).

---

9 Read the first paragraph. **Find** and **copy two** words that show Basher Beaumont made the narrator's life miserable.

_____

1 mark

10 Give **two** reasons the narrator says he had been *more miserable than I had ever been* in the second paragraph.

1. _____

_____

2. _____

_____

2 marks

11 *I picked at the plaster in the wall, and determined there and then that I would run away.*

✓ Tick **one** word that could replace the word *determined* in that sentence.

broke ☐   decided ☐   courage ☐

1 mark

12 Read about the narrator's escape.

Put ticks (✓) in the table to show which of these are **true** and which are **false**.

	True	False
He ran as fast as he could.		
He was being chased by dogs.		
He ran five miles to the station.		
He climbed a tree and hid in it.		

2 marks

13 Number the sentences below from **1** to **4** to show the order of the narrator's escape plan.

Climb the fence. ☐

Explain to his family. ☐

Walk to the station. ☐

Catch a train. ☐

1 mark

14 Why do you think his mother's letter made him feel homesick?

✓ Tick **one**.

He didn't like semolina pudding. ☐

His mother frightened him. ☐

He realised how much he preferred home. ☐

Basher stole his letter. ☐

1 mark

15 The boy in the story will have to explain to his parents why he is *never, ever going back*.

Complete what you think he might say to convince them.

"You need to listen to me …

_____

_____

_____

_____

2 marks

Nerves of Steel

by Josh Lury

A lonely microphone waits
At the front of the stage.

I peek out from behind the curtains –
A million pairs of eyes are waiting too.

A piece of paper trembles in my hands
As if the paper is the one that is scared.

I imagine how a young warrior felt
Before his first battle.

Did his sword shake and rattle
From nerves of steel?

Or the orphan who dared to ask for more.
Did the spoon chatter in its empty bowl?

What about the first man on the moon
Just before the hatch opened?

Did the space boots tap and jiggle
In a dance of anxiety?

Or the flag pole wobble in his hand
While he tried to plant it in the grey dust?

And then I remember Gran
And how she used to say

What doesn't kill you
Will only make you stronger.

And I took one small step for a boy
Then one giant leap onto the stage

And recited my poem in front of a million eyes.
This poem.

It didn't kill me and, yes, I think Gran was right.
I do feel a little bit stronger.

Tourist Information

What to do during your visit

Welcome to our town. You have chosen an excellent destination for your holiday, and can choose from any number of great activities. Here are just some:

Follow the Zebra Trail

The River Zeb flows through the town and out towards the coast. The Zebra trail is a specially widened footpath that allows cyclists and walkers to enjoy the splendid views in peace. Follow the black and white signposts to stay on the Zebra Trail for a tranquil evening walk.

Why not hire bikes from Jen's Bike hire, and head out of town for a relaxing and traffic-free ride along the banks of the river? You can stop and look for wildlife such as kingfishers, otters or perhaps even a reclusive badger, though it is unlikely you will actually see a zebra.

Unearth the mystery

Visit the site of the ancient ruins for a day of mystery and history. The site was first uncovered in 1944, when a WW2 bomb landed and the crater exposed some unusual coins.

Since then, archaeologists have discovered objects going back in history to before the time of the Romans. Some think that this may in fact be the true site of King Arthur's Camelot.

Many local enthusiasts spend their time using metal detectors to help the search.

You can even have a go at being an archaeologist yourself, by digging with expert supervision. Will you find a Roman coin, or some ancient pottery? Perhaps you will be the one to unearth Arthur's famous sword, Excalibur.

Quiet please!

If you want to escape the hustle and bustle, why not visit the library? This isn't any ordinary library – it was voted the *Quietest Place in Great Britain* for three years in a row.

Ever since it opened in 1912, this has been a place where even whispers sound like the roaring of a hurricane. It is said that the noisiest event in its history was in 1984, when a pin dropped onto the hard floor. Since then, carpets have been fitted to ensure absolute silence.

Name: Class: Date:

Questions 1–8 are about 'Nerves of Steel' (pages 24–25).

1 The poet says that *a million pairs of eyes* are waiting.

Which of these **best** explains why the poet used the word *million*?

✓ Tick **one**.

A million people were in the audience. ☐

To exaggerate and show the feeling. ☐

To show the poet can count well. ☐

It was on television. ☐

_____
1 mark

2 The poet compares his nerves with three other kinds of people.

Tick to show the **three** people whose nerves the poet describes.

✓ Tick **three**.

an astronaut ☐

his gran ☐

the audience ☐

an orphan ☐

a warrior ☐

_____
1 mark

3 Why is the title *Nerves of Steel* suitable for the whole poem?

_____

_____

_____

1 mark

4 **a)** How does the poet show that the orphan is still hungry?

_____

_____

1 mark

b) How does the poet show that the orphan is brave?

_____

_____

1 mark

5 **Find** and **copy two** phrases that show how different objects show someone is worried.

1. _____

_____

2. _____

_____

2 marks

6 Draw **four** lines to match each word from the poem with its meaning.

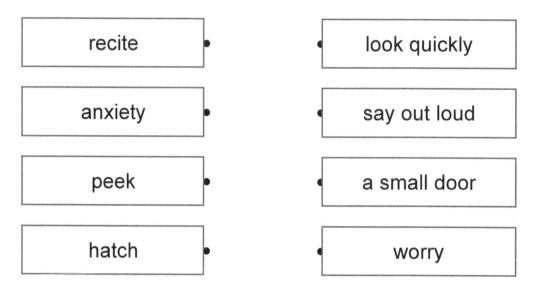

recite	look quickly
anxiety	say out loud
peek	a small door
hatch	worry

2 marks

7 The poet's gran says *What doesn't kill you / Will only make you stronger*.

How does this explain the end of the poem?

_____

_____

_____

1 mark

8 Put ticks (✓) in the table to show which of these are **true** and which are **false**.

	True	False
The poem uses rhymes in every verse.		
The poem has two lines in each verse.		
The poem is mainly about what it is like to watch a school play.		

1 mark

Questions 9–15 are about **Tourist Information** (pages 26–27).

9   The title is *Tourist Information*. What is a *tourist*?

_____

_____

1 mark

10   **Find** and **copy** the names of **three** creatures you might see by the river.

_____   _____

_____

1 mark

11   Find the word *tranquil* in the text. Which word below could replace it and keep a similar meaning?

✓ Tick **one**.

difficult ☐   loud ☐   peaceful ☐

1 mark

12   Why is the title *Unearth the mystery* suitable for the second section?

_____

_____

_____

_____

2 marks

13 Read the paragraph about the ruins.

Put ticks (✓) in the table to show which of these are **true** and which are **false**.

	True	False
The ruins were destroyed by bombs.		
They use explosives to find more ruins.		
The bombs were the reason that the ruins were first discovered.		

1 mark

14 Explain why this particular library is such a good place to *escape the hustle and bustle*.

_____

_____

1 mark

15 Which visitor attraction would you prefer to visit?
Use information from the text to explain your choice.

I would prefer to visit the _____

because _____

_____

_____

2 marks

From *Your Brain*

by Sally Morgan

The control centre

Your brain is the control centre of your body. It works 24 hours a day, seven days a week for the whole of your life, even when you're sleeping.

Controls and checks

Your brain controls everything that's going on in your body. It makes lots of checks too, to be certain that all is working properly. It tells you when you're hungry, tired or in pain. It makes sure that you breathe and that your heart keeps pumping. It's also the place where you do all your thinking and store your memories.

Our brain is the most advanced in the animal kingdom. It allows us to do things many other animals can't, such as read, write and learn languages.

Many cells

Your brain is found inside your head. It's a surprisingly large organ. An adult's brain weighs about 1.4 kilograms. It's very soft and pinky-white on the outside and grey-white inside.

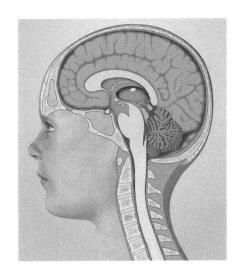

Your brain is made up of billions of cells. Cells are the tiniest part of your body, so small that you can't see them. There are many different types of cell in your body, each designed to do a particular job. For example, there are red blood cells that carry oxygen around your body, bone cells that make up your bones, skin cells that form a covering for your body and liver cells that make bile, a liquid that helps to break down your food.

There is fat and water in your brain too, but no blood. Instead, your brain is surrounded by blood vessels. Blood flows around your body in blood vessels. The blood brings food and oxygen to your brain.

Large head

Newborn babies have large heads for their size. This is because they are born with brains that are almost full size. As they get older, their body grows, so their head does not look as large.

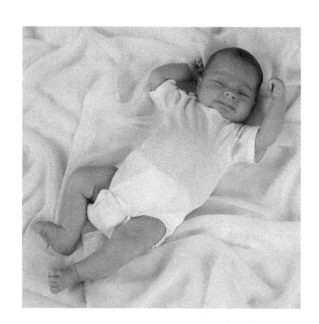

On the road to Lonesome Lake

From *Little Wolf's Book of Badness*
by Ian Whybrow

Day 1 – morning

Dear Mum and Dad,

Please please PLEEEEEZ let me come home. I have been walking and walking all day, and guess how far? Not even ten miles, I bet. I have not even reached Lonesome Lake yet. You know I hate going on adventures. So why do I have to go hundreds of miles to Uncle Bigbad's school in the middle of a dark damp forest?

You say you do not get on in life these days without a BAD badge. But I know loads of really bad wolves who never went to school. Ever. Like my cousin Yeller for one. I know you want me to be wild and wicked like Dad, but why do I have to go so far away? Just what is so wonderful about Cunning College in Frettnin Forest? And what is so brilliant about having Uncle Bigbad as a teacher? Is it all because Dad went to Brutal Hall and they made him a prefect and he got a silver BAD badge when he left? I bet it is.

There is another four days' walk, maybe more to Frettnin Forest. Let me come back and learn to be bad at home.

PLEE-EE-EEZ!!!

Your number 1 cub,

Little Wolf

PS Don't forget to say Hello baby bruv to Smellybreff and tell him not to touch any of my things.

Name: Class: Date:

Questions 1–9 are about *Your Brain* (pages 33–34).

---

1   Read the first paragraph.

Put ticks (✓) in the table to show which of these are **true** and which are **false**.

	True	False
The brain works non-stop.		
The brain is not active during sleep.		
The brain only works during the day.		

1 mark

---

2   Read the second paragraph.

Find **two** different functions that show the brain is vital for keeping us alive.

1. _____

2. _____

2 marks

---

3   **Find** and **copy** a phrase that shows the human brain is more powerful than other creatures' brains.

_____

1 mark

---

4 Find the description of cells.

Which word **best** describes them?

✓ Tick **one**.

expensive ☐

intelligent ☐

bone ☐

microscopic ☐

1 mark

5 **Find** and **copy** the word that describes how blood moves around the body.

_____

1 mark

6 The text states that the brain *is a surprisingly large organ.*

What does this tell us about the brain? Put ticks (✓) in the table to show which statements are **true** and which are **false**.

	True	False
No one knows how big the brain is.		
The brain is larger than you might expect it to be.		
The brain is actually smaller than most people think it is.		
Readers might be amazed to learn about the size of the brain.		

2 marks

7 Why do babies seem to have large heads?

_____

_____

1 mark

8 Draw **four** lines to match the cell type to its job.

bone cells	•	•	build and repair the covering of the body
red blood cells	•	•	manufacture bile for digestion
liver cells	•	•	construct the skeleton
skin cells	•	•	transport oxygen

1 mark

9 How is the brain supplied with food and oxygen?

✓ Tick **one**.

from blood vessels inside the brain ☐

through the nose ☐

in the bile ☐

from blood vessels outside the brain ☐

1 mark

> Questions 10–15 are about
> 'On the road to Lonesome Lake' (page 35).

10 **Find** and **copy two** phrases that show this is a letter.

1. _____

_____

2. _____

_____

2 marks

11 **Find** and **copy** a word that shows Little Wolf's Dad had been energetic when he was at school.

_____

1 mark

12 Little Wolf writes *Please please PLEEEEEZ* and *PLEE-EE-EEZ!!!*

Put ticks (✓) in the table to show which of these are **true** and which are **false**.

	True	False
He is desperate not to go to the new school.		
He really wants to start soon.		
He is trying to convince his parents.		

1 mark

13 Little Wolf writes about his cousin Yeller.

What does he hope this will prove?

_____

_____

_____

_____

2 marks

14 Number the sentences below from **1** to **4** to show the order Little Wolf uses them to try to persuade his parents.

You can learn outside school. ☐

He has too far to walk. ☐

He misses his brother. ☐

He does not need to be just like his dad. ☐

1 mark

15 Imagine Little Wolf's mother writes a letter back to him. Complete her letter, including some details from the text.

Dear Little Wolf,

I know you are not happy at the moment, but you can do it. I believe in you …

_____

_____

_____

2 marks

From *Mr Stink*

by David Walliams

Mr Stink gave a resigned smile. He reached into his jacket pocket and slowly withdrew the spoon, then handed it to her. Chloe turned it over in her hands. Looking at it close up, she realised she'd been wrong. It wasn't three letters engraved on it. It was a single letter on a crest, held on each side by a lion.

A single, capital letter D.

"You are Lord Darlington," said Chloe. "Let me see that old photograph again."

Mr Stink carefully pulled out his old black and white photograph.

Chloe studied it for a few seconds. It was just as she'd remembered. The beautiful young couple, the Rolls Royce, the stately home. Only now, when she looked at it, she could see the resemblance between the young man in the photo and the old tramp beside her.

"And that's you in the picture." Chloe held the photograph delicately, knowing she was handling something very precious. Mr Stink looked much younger, especially without his beard and dirt. But the eyes were sparkling. It was unmistakably him.

"The game's up," said Mr Stink. "That is me, Chloe. A lifetime ago."

"And who's this lady with you?"

"My wife."

"Your wife? I didn't know you were married."

"You didn't know I was a lord, either," said Mr Stink.

"And that must be your house then, Lord Darlington," said Chloe, indicating the stately home standing behind the couple in the photograph. Mr Stink nodded. "Well then, how come you're homeless now?"

"It's a long story, my dear," said Mr Stink, evasively.

"But I want to hear it," said Chloe. "Please? I've told you so much about my life. And I've always wanted to know your story, Mr Stink, ever since I first saw you. I always knew you must have a fascinating tale to tell."

Mr Stink took a breath. "Well, I had it all, child. More money than I could ever spend, a beautiful house with its own lake. My life was like an endless summer. Croquet, tea on the lawn, long lion days spent playing cricket. And to make things even more perfect I married this beautiful, clever, funny, adorable woman, my childhood sweetheart. Violet."

Invisible Noise

by Josh Lury

I stepped outside on the tops of the tips of my tiptoes

Silently.

I crept out into the sun's last soft rays

And I was quieter than a mouse's blink,

Or the crash of a feather landing.

It was like being invisible in sound.

And then everything came to my ears:

I heard the light sparkle off a raindrop

Broken and jingling like smashed glass.

I caught the whoosh of a tornado

Swirling off the edge of a butterfly's wing

Like a whirlpool

As it came in to land on a leaf.

And at my quietest,

At the moment when even the electricity

In my brain became still

I thought I could hear the rubbery squeak

Of a blade of grass growing

A hundredth of a thousandth

Of a millionth of a centimetre.

But then I heard them –

The hammering hoofbeats of a hundred horses

Galloping across the grass towards me.

The thundering beasts hurtling and trampling.

Every way I twisted

To look for this new invisible din

I heard only more invisible noise growing louder

As if it was already inside my chest

Beating to get out.

And I realised

The hoofbeats

Were heartbeats.

And I remembered to stop holding my breath.

Name:	Class:	Date:

> Questions 1–9 are about *Mr Stink* (pages 41–42).

1 What led Chloe to believe that Mr Stink was really Lord Darlington?

_____

1 mark

2 **Find** and **copy two** phrases that show details Chloe can see in the photograph.

1. _____

_____

2. _____

_____

2 marks

3 Find the part in the story where Chloe studies the photograph.

Put ticks (✓) in the table to show which of these are **true** and which are **false**.

	True	False
The photograph sparkled because it was made from precious jewels.		
The photograph was old and delicate.		
The photograph held a secret story.		

2 marks

4 Who was Violet?

Find **two** statements that describe her.

✓ Tick **two**.

the lady in the photograph ☐

Chloe's mum ☐

the lady who discovered his real identity ☐

Mr Stink's childhood sweetheart ☐

1 mark

5 Mr Stink says *"The game's up."*

Explain what he means by this.

_____

_____

_____

2 marks

6 Which word used by the author shows that Mr Stink was reluctant to tell the true story.

✓ Tick **one**.

evasively ☐   fascinating ☐   withdrew ☐

1 mark

7 Mr Stink once lived a rich and perfect life. Find evidence from the text that show his lifestyle was now very different.

_____

_____

1 mark

8 Mr Stink uses the phrase *long lion days*.

Which statement **best** explains the meaning of this phrase?

✓ Tick **one**.

relaxing summer days ☐

days spent hunting ☐

days when his hair was like a mane ☐

long cold nights with a frost as sharp as claws ☐

1 mark

9 Imagine you are Chloe, listening to the story of his youth. What **question** would you ask next? Explain why.

_____

_____

_____

_____

2 marks

Questions 10–15 are about 'Invisible Noise'
(pages 43–44).

10 The poet *stepped outside on the tops of the tips of my tiptoes.*

Which of the following **best** explains why the poet walks like this?

✓ Tick **one**.

to see over the garden fence ☐

to tread noiselessly ☐

so the horses won't stamp on the poet's toes ☐

because there was smashed glass on the path ☐

1 mark

11 **Find** and **copy** the phrase that shows the poem is set in the evening.

_____

1 mark

12 Find the line which first describes the horses. What do you notice about the poet's choice of words in that line?

_____

_____

1 mark

13 **Find** and **copy** the phrase that describes a very small amount of growth.

_____

_____

1 mark

14 Does the poet hear horses?

Explain, using information from the poem.

_____

_____

_____

_____

2 marks

15 **Find** and **copy** a phrase that the poet uses to make it seem as if you can hear light.

_____

_____

1 mark

Like a Red Rag to a Goat

A charity fundraiser ended in excitement last week at a local school as Lizzie, a prize goat, caused havoc. The Hampton Junior School fair, which is held annually, came to a surprising end when the goat escaped her enclosure and ran amok through the school field.

Lizzie is a prize nanny goat. A nanny is the name for a female goat.

Initially, the fair had been a huge success, with many children, parents, grandparents and locals enjoying a range of activities. including a penalty shoot-out competition, face painting, tombola and much more. Due to a forecast of high winds the bouncy castle had to be cancelled, which disappointed many children.

One traditional event was the 'Guess the Weight' stall, which has been run by a local farmer, Mike Peters, for 25 years, since taking over the farm from his own father. Every year they bring one of the farm animals to graze in a corner of the field while people take it in turns to guess the animal's weight. The closest estimate wins a prize of a ride in the vintage tractor for the parade at the end of the fair.

The problem began when Nathan Jones, father of Millie Jones in Class 4, decided it would be amusing to have his face painted to look like a tomato. The smile was wiped from his face when he took Millie to Farmer Peter's stall. Lizzie, who is normally a calm and gentle creature, took one look at the red-faced father-of-three and broke out of her pen and hurtled after the alarmed Mr Jones.

"I was terrified," said Nathan, 30. "I grabbed my daughter and climbed right to the top of the climbing frame, where we had to wait to be rescued."

He added that it was like "being chased by a monster in a nightmare. I wanted to run but my legs just wouldn't move."

When asked to comment, Farmer Peters looked amused. "She wouldn't have done him any harm. She loves tomatoes and probably just wanted to sniff his face."

Lizzie, a horned goat of 140 pounds in weight, had to be coaxed away by headteacher Ms Trounce and the appropriately named Mr Billy Kidd, Mayor of Hampton, who had come to open the fair by cutting the ribbon with his giant pair of scissors.

The day ended with smiles all round when Ms Trounce announced that the winner of the Guess the Weight competition was none other than Millie Jones of Class 4.

From *A Dog Called Homeless*

by Sarah Lean

More rain gushed down the windows, filled up the drains and made great puddles and ponds in the road and on the common. Mrs Cooper said, "Absolutely not in this weather," when Sam asked if we could go to the common. We wanted to find Homeless and make sure he was safe; find Jed and ask him, somehow, about Mum.

"I don't ever remember so much rain," Mrs Cooper said, looking into the sky, "not this time of year. The river in town will burst its banks if it carries on like this. And besides, you can't go out, you've got another hospital appointment later, Sam."

We sat together on the window seat, played hand-clapping games.

"What is a ghost?" Sam tapped on my hand.

"A dead person come back," I spelled.

"Can you touch them or smell them?"

"No, you can only see them. But you can sort of hear them, like a ..."

I realised Sam wouldn't understand TV because he couldn't hear or see one. The Coopers didn't even have a television set.

"You know what a telephone is?" I spelled.

Sam smiled and put his hand by his ear, pretended he was holding one. He explained he could tell when the telephone was ringing. They had a telephone with really big numbers. It rang like a bell and buzzed so Sam could feel the vibrations. He spelled that sometimes his mum gave him messages from people who rang up.

"A bit like that," I tapped.

You can tell when Sam is trying to work things out or remember something. He hangs his head; his long black fringe falls over his face. The only thing that moves is his bony-thin chest and you can just hear a little wheeze at the end of his quick breathing.

"Like a message," he spelled. He leaned back. "Can you phone them?" he tapped.

Sam isn't like ordinary people. He thinks about things differently. Maybe it's because he can't see or hear, but sometimes what he said just made me feel like my brain and heart were exploding. In a good way. I wanted to tell him he was magic because he made me feel like I wasn't weird or mad or stupid.

Name: Class: Date:

Questions 1–8 are about **'Like a Red Rag to a Goat'**
(pages 50–51).

1 Read the opening sentence of the newspaper report.

Which word has the same meaning as *havoc*?

✓ Tick **one**.

victory ☐

vacuum ☐

mayhem ☐

heavy ☐

1 mark

2 List **two** activities that took place, other than the *Guess the Weight* activity.

1. _____

2. _____

2 marks

3 What did Millie's father do that caused the problem?

_____

1 mark

4 What information does the caption tell the reader?

_____

1 mark

5 Draw **four** lines to match the name to the action they performed.

Mike		climbed the climbing frame
Ms Trounce		opened the fundraiser
Nathan		announced the winner
Mr Kidd		ran a stall

1 mark

6 Explain what caused the day to end *with smiles all round*.

_____

_____

_____

2 marks

7 Number the sentences below from **1** to **4** to show the order in which they happened.

The mayor helped take Lizzie away. ☐

The bouncy castle was cancelled. ☐

The winner was announced. ☐

Millie's father approached Lizzie. ☐

1 mark

8 Which of these are usually features of a newspaper report.

✓ Tick **two**.

headline ☐

fiction ☐

quotations ☐

signature ☐

1 mark

Questions 9–15 are about
A Dog called Homeless (pages 52–53).

9 List **two** reasons Mrs Cooper gives for them not being allowed to go out.

1. _____

_____

2. _____

_____

2 marks

10 Explain why they communicate using hand taps.

_____

_____

1 mark

11 Which word **best** describes the narrator's feelings for Sam?

✓ Tick **one**.

admiration ☐

confusion ☐

curiosity ☐

sympathy ☐

1 mark

12 Read the paragraph beginning *You can tell when …*

Find and **copy two** phrases that demonstrate Sam's poor health.

1. _____

_____

2. _____

_____

2 marks

13 Read the description of the weather in the first paragraph. Explain the meaning of the word *great* in this description.

_____

_____

1 mark

14 The narrator says Sam *made me feel like my brain and heart were exploding. In a good way.*

Put ticks (✓) in the table to show which of these are **true** and which are **false**.

	True	False
This is because Sam makes the narrator feel more self-confident.		
This is because Sam makes the narrator feel so sorry for him.		
This is because the narrator knows Sam cannot see ghosts.		
This is because Sam had learned how to use the telephone.		

2 marks

15 Write a question you think they might ask Jed next time they see him.

_____

_____

_____

1 mark

Mark scheme for Autumn Half Term Test 1

Qu.	Content Domain	Requirement	Mark
		'The Dragon and His Granny'	
1	2g	**Award 1 mark** for *Times were tough*.	1
2	2a	**Award 1 mark** for adventurous.	1
3	2a	**Award 1 mark** for somewhat.	1
4	2d	**Award 1 mark** for a basic answer referring to the following facts: they were cold; they were hungry; they didn't have a home. **Award 2 marks** for an answer that develops this into an explanation, e.g. It was winter and they did not have a home, so they thought they might freeze or starve.	2
5	2d	**Award 1 mark** for all 3 correct: The dragon was hiding – False. The dragon was trying to trick the boys – True. The boys began to trust the dragon – True.	1
6	2d	**Award 1 mark** for an answer that refers to the dragon being mean or evil. **Award 2 marks** for an answer that explains how the dragon had pretended to be kind and helpful, but now showed that he was mean – had tricked the boys.	2
7	2a	**Award 1 mark** for a cost to their freedom.	1
8	2c	**Award 1 mark** for all 4 correct: 1 = They are determined to find a new life. 2 = They are afraid they won't survive the winter. 3 = They trust the dragon. 4 = They feel deceived.	1
9	2e	**Award 1 mark** for an answer that refers to the involvement of the dragon's granny. **Award 1 mark** for an answer that refers to the boys' attempts to free themselves from the dragon's trick.	2
		'Telescopes'	
10	2b	**Award 1 mark** for: (around) 500 years ago.	1
11	2a	**Award 1 mark** for a direct quote that includes *study stars and planets*.	1
12	2d	**Award 1 mark** for correct option: To avoid pollution.	1
13	2b	**Award 1 mark each** for any 2 of the following: • It is in space; it orbits the earth. • It can see further than other telescopes; it sends back clear pictures of the stars. • It has been operating for more than 20 years.	2
14	2g	**Award 1 mark** for reference to **both** its large size and the fact it is European.	1
15	2d	**Award 2 marks for** an answer that explains how people had thought the Earth was the centre of the universe for a very long time (thousands of years), but that Galileo showed this was not true. **Award 1 mark** for an answer that refers to Galileo's idea, but does not fully explain why it was shocking or surprising.	2
		TOTAL MARKS	**20**

Mark scheme for Autumn Half Term Test 2

Qu.	Content Domain	Requirement	Mark
		'Paris'	
1	2b	**Award 1 mark** for answer that indicates it is a hill in Paris, but most of Paris is flat.	1
2	2b	**Award 1 mark** for *The shells and bones of sea creatures*.	1
3	2b	**Award 1 mark** for Romans.	1
4	2a	**Award 1 mark** for both correct: visit Paris each year – over 15 million live permanently – over 2.2 million.	1
5	2g	**Award 1 mark** for winds.	1
6	2c	**Award 1 mark** for numbers in the following order: 1 = Parisi 2 = Romans 3 = Vietnamese immigrants	1
7	2c	**Award 2 marks** for all four correct; **award 1 mark** for 2 or 3 correct: The Romans named the town the Île de la Cité – False. Modern Paris has 37 bridges – True. Lutetia was built around the islands – True. Notre Dame is built beneath the city – False.	2
8	2b, 2d	**Award 1 mark each** for any 2 plausible answers based on the text, e.g. • to buy fruits like durian and rambutan that are not available anywhere else • to eat in the Chinese and Vietnamese restaurants • to live in the high-rise flats • because it's very busy and exciting.	2
		The Butterfly Lion	
9	2g	**Award 1 mark** for any 2 of: *terrorised*; *tormented*; *dread*.	1
10	2d	**Award 1 mark each** for any 2 from: homesick after letter; attack by Basher; punished by Mr Carter.	2
11	2a	**Award 1 mark** for decided.	1
12	2c, 2g	**Award 2 marks** for all 4 correct; **award 1 mark** for 2 or 3 correct: He ran as fast as he could – True. He was being chased by dogs – False. He ran five miles to the station – False. He climbed a tree and hid in it – False.	2
13	2c	**Award 1 mark** for numbers in the following order: 1 = Climb the fence. 3 = Catch a train. 2 = Walk to the station. 4 = Explain to his family.	1
14	2d	**Award 1 mark** for: He realised how much he preferred home.	1
15	2b, 2d	**Award 2 marks for** an answer that gives at least 2 reasons based on the text, or that links events to feelings and emotions, or gives reasons to stay with the family as well as reasons not to return. **Award 1 mark** for an undeveloped answer, e.g. that shows 1 reason or feeling.	2
		TOTAL MARKS	**20**

Mark scheme for Spring Half Term Test 1

Qu.	Content Domain	Requirement	Mark
		'Nerves of Steel'	
1	2g	**Award 1 mark** for: To exaggerate and show the feeling.	1
2	2b	**Award 1 mark** for all 3 correct options chosen: astronaut, orphan, warrior.	1
3	2c	**Award 1 mark** for an answer that indicates the poem is about feeling nervous or worried about a performance. Do not accept an answer that refers to only one part, e.g. the astronaut.	1
4	2d	**Award 1 mark** for an answer that refers to the empty bowl, or asking for more. **Award 1 mark** for an answer that refers to the word *dared* in the poem.	2
5	2d	**Award 1 mark each** for any 2 from: paper trembling; sword shaking/rattling; spoon chattering; space boots jiggling/tapping; flagpole wobbling.	2
6	2a	**Award 2 marks** for all 4 correct; **award 1 mark** for 2 or 3 correct: recite – say out loud; anxiety – worry; peek – a quick look; hatch – a small door.	2
7	2c, 2d	**Award 1 mark** for an answer that refers to the fact that the poet had been nervous, but overcame the fears/met the challenge, and now feels better.	1
8	2a, 2c	**Award 1 mark** for all three correct: The poem uses rhymes in every verse – False. The poem has two lines in each verse – True. The poem is mainly about what it is like to watch a school play – False.	1
		Tourist Information	
9	2a	**Award 1 mark** for an answer that indicates a kind of visitor or someone on holiday.	1
10	2b	**Award 1 mark** for reference to otter, kingfisher and badger. Do not accept zebra.	1
11	2a	**Award 1 mark** for peaceful.	1
12	2g	**Award 2 marks** for an answer that explains the link between unknown or mysterious objects being hidden underground and having opportunities to discover them. **Award 1 mark** for an answer that explains the meaning of only unearth, or mystery.	2
13	2b	**Award 1 mark** for all three correct: The ruins were destroyed by bombs – False. They use explosives to find more ruins – False. The bombs were the reason that the ruins were first discovered – True.	1
14	2b	**Award 1 mark** for an answer that demonstrates the pupil has understood that it is an especially quiet place, perhaps mentioning the awards. Do not accept a generic answer, e.g. libraries are always quiet and peaceful.	1
15	2b	**Award 2 marks** for an answer that explains the choice with personal reasons supported by information given in the text, e.g. I would go to the ruins because I am very interested in King Arthur and people think the ruins may be the site of Camelot. **Award 1 mark** for an answer that gives information from the text but does not indicate why it links to their own preference, e.g. I would go to the library because it is quiet.	2
		TOTAL MARKS	**20**

Mark scheme for Spring Half Term Test 2

Qu.	Content Domain	Requirement	Mark
		Your Brain	
1	2b	**Award 1 mark** for all 3 correct: The brain works non-stop – True. The brain is not active during sleep – False. The brain only works during the day – False.	1
2	2b	**Award 1 mark each** for any 2 from: • tells you when you're hungry/tired/in pain • makes sure you breathe • makes sure your heart keeps pumping	2
3	2b	**Award 1 mark** for either of the following: • *Our brain is the most advanced in the animal kingdom.* • *It allows us to do things many other animals can't, such as read, write and learn languages.*	1
4	2a	**Award 1 mark** for microscopic.	1
5	2d	**Award 1 mark** for *flows*. Also accept *pumps*.	1
6	2g	**Award 2 marks** for all 4 correct; **award 1 mark** for 3 correct: No one knows how big the brain is – False. The brain is larger than you might expect it to be – True. The brain is actually smaller than most people think it is – False. Readers might be amazed to learn about the size of the brain – True.	2
7	2c	**Award 1 mark** for an answer that indicates either that babies are born with brains almost fully grown; or their bodies grow more than their brains as they grow up.	1
8	2b	**Award 1 mark** for all four correctly matched: bone cells – construct the skeleton red blood cells – transport oxygen liver cells – manufacture bile for digestion skin cells – build and repair the covering of the body.	1
9	2b	**Award 1 mark** for: from blood vessels outside the brain.	1
		'On the road to Lonesome Lake'	
10	2g	**Award 1 mark each** for any 2 from the following: • *Dear Mum and Dad* • *Your number 1 cub* • *PS …* Also accept reference to the date: *Day 1 – morning.*	2
11	2a	**Award 1 mark** for *wild*. Do not accept *wicked*.	1
12	2d	**Award 1 mark** for all 3 correct: He is desperate not to go to the new school – True. He really wants to start soon – False. He is trying to convince his parents – True.	1

Qu.	Content Domain	Requirement	Mark
13	2d	**Award 2 marks** for an answer that explains fully that Yeller did not go to school but still manages to be a bad wolf (i.e. live up to their hopes). **Award 1 mark** for an answer that gives a partial explanation, e.g. Yeller didn't go to school.	2
14	2c	**Award 1 mark** for numbers in the correct order: 2,1,4,3. 1 = He has too far to walk. 2 = You can learn outside school. 3 = He does not need to be just like his dad. 4 = He misses his brother.	1
15	2e	**Award 2 marks** for a full answer that includes encouragement alongside information from the text, e.g. 'You can be even better than your cousin' or 'Your Dad felt the same too when he went'. **Award 1 mark** for an answer that is just general encouragement or that gives a brief answer such as 'Your dad did it too'.	2
		TOTAL MARKS	20

Mark scheme for Summer Half Term Test 1

Qu.	Content Domain	Requirement	Mark
		Mr Stink	
1	2d	**Award 1 mark** for either of the following: the spoon; the photograph.	1
2	2b	**Award 1 mark each** for any 2 of: *The beautiful young couple*; *the Rolls Royce*; *the stately home*. Also accept: *Mr Stink looked much younger*; *the eyes were sparkling*.	2
3	2g	**Award 2 marks** for all 3 correct; **award 1 mark** for 2 correct: The photograph sparkled because it was made from precious jewels – False. The photograph was old and delicate – True. The photograph held a secret story – True.	2
4	2b	**Award 1 mark** for 2 options correctly chosen: • the lady in the photograph • Mr Stink's childhood sweetheart.	1
5	2d	**Award 2 marks** for an answer that explains fully the fact that Mr Stink had been keeping a secret for years, but that Chloe had now found the truth so he no longer needed to keep the secret. **Award 1 mark** for a partial explanation, e.g. he was keeping a secret.	2
6	2a	**Award 1 mark** for *evasively*.	1
7	2c	**Award 1 mark** for an answer that refers either to homelessness or to his dirty beard/ rough appearance.	1
8	2g	**Award 1 mark** for relaxing summer days.	1
9	2e	**Award 2 marks** for a question and explanation that show a desire to find out how Mr Stink has gone from a perfect life to his current circumstances. **Award 1 mark** for a question that prompts more of the story, but only in general terms, or a question with no explanation of why it would be asked.	2
		'Invisible Noise'	
10	2g	**Award 1 mark** for to tread noiselessly.	1
11	2a	**Award 1 mark** for an answer that includes the phrase *the sun's last soft rays*.	1
12	2g	**Award 1 mark** for an answer that notices the repetition of the letter *h*, and may include the word 'alliteration'.	1
13	2a, 2d	Award 1 mark for an answer that includes: *a hundredth of a thousandth of a millionth of a centimetre*.	1
14	2c	**Award 2 marks** for an answer that indicates that the poet seems to hear horses but then finds out it is actually the sound of their own heartbeat, which was loud because they had been holding their breath, or because they had been so silent even that sounded loud. **Award 1 mark** for a partial answer, e.g. no, it was heartbeats.	2
15	2d	**Award 1 mark** for the phrase *I heard the light sparkle off a raindrop*. Also accept *Broken and jingling like smashed glass*.	1
		TOTAL MARKS	**20**

Mark scheme for Summer Half Term Test 2

Qu.	Content Domain	Requirement	Mark
		'Like a Red Rag to a Goat'	
1	2a	**Award 1 mark** for mayhem.	1
2	2b	**Award 1 mark each** for any 2 from: a penalty shoot-out competition, face painting, tombola. Do not accept bouncy castle.	2
3	2b	**Award 1 mark** for answer that refers to having his face painted red.	1
4	2g	**Award 1 mark** for answer that refers to the name for a female goat being *nanny*. Also accept answers that refer to the information that Lizzie is a prize goat or nanny.	1
5	2c	**Award 1 mark** for all 4 lines correct: Mike – ran a stall Ms Trounce – announced the winner Nathan – climbed the climbing frame Mr Kidd – opened the fundraiser.	1
6	2g	**Award 2 marks** for an answer that shows understanding that Millie won the competition and this was funny for everyone because she had been chased by Lizzie. **Award 1 mark** for a partial answer, e.g. because Millie won.	2
7	2c	**Award 1 mark** for all 4 items in the correct order: 1 = The bouncy castle was cancelled. 2 = Millie's father approached Lizzie. 3 = The mayor helped take Lizzie away. 4 = The winner was announced.	1
8	2b	**Award 1 mark** for the 2 correct options: headline; quotations.	1
		A Dog Called Homeless	
9	2a	**Award 1 mark** for bad weather/rain and **1 mark** for hospital appointment,	2
10	2g	**Award 1 mark** for an answer that refers to the fact that Sam is blind and deaf.	1
11	2a	**Award 1 mark** for admiration.	1
12	2d	**Award 1 mark each** for any 2 from: • *his bony-thin chest* • *a little wheeze* • *his quick breathing.*	2
13	2a	**Award 1 mark** for an answer that explains it means large/big.	1
14	2c	**Award 2 marks** for all 4 correct; **award 1 mark** for 3 correct: This is because Sam makes the narrator feel more self-confident – True. This is because Sam makes the narrator feel so sorry for him – False. This is because the narrator knows Sam cannot see ghosts – False. This is because Sam had learned how to use the telephone – False.	2
15	2e	**Award 1 mark** for an answer that either asks about Mum or refers to another plausible detail from the text, such as *Have you seen Homeless?*	1
		TOTAL MARKS	20

Name:	Class:

Year 4 Reading Comprehension Record Sheet

Tests	Mark	Total marks	Key skills to target
Autumn Half Term Test 1			
Autumn Half Term Test 2			
Spring Half Term Test 1			
Spring Half Term Test 2			
Summer Half Term Test 1			
Summer Half Term Test 2			